Employment Law and

(Individual employment law)

Volume 1

Part 1

The employment relationship

Part 2

Termination of employment

Questions and suggested answers

Written by Steve J Norton

LLB,GDL,MA,MRES, LPC

Dedicated to Leah and Barbara

Acknowledgements

I have drawn on a number of sources in drafting this book. These include range from the LPC CLP practice guide on Employment Law and Practice, through to useful guides produced by organisations like the Law Express series of books[i], and also the Labour Research Dept. I have referenced these texts. I have also used web source information as employment law is constantly changing and I have tried to provide the most current information.

INTRODUCTION

I wrote this book as an aid to those like me who have studied this subject area as an elective on the Legal Practice Course (LPC) or similar courses combining theory and practical application. I have tried to produce a number of questions and suggested answers based on information from my own notes and studies which I hope existing or potential or existing LPC students will find useful as a study guide which is based around typical exam type questions.

I have produced 3 volumes and dealt with two areas of employment law and practice in each one. In this first volume I have included questions and suggested answers on two areas of employment law. Part 1 deals with the nature of the employment relationship. In Part 2 I have set questions with suggested answers on the issue of the various types of termination or dismissal. I appreciate there are many books out there are many revision books on employment law that cover the same areas . However, my purpose is to use this book as a way of seeing how problem scenarios are set and ways of looking at finding solutions. This is the bread and butter for trainee lawyers and trade union case workers, or human resource specialists who deal with employment or workplace cases. As many people working in the area of employment law know, the law is constantly changing and books written in 2017 or 2018 are now already out of date with some key appeal judgments only decided at the end of 2018, such as Uber and Pimlico Plumbers. I have included these outcomes in questions and suggested answers on the `gig economy'.

I hope you find this book useful as an aid to your studies or general interest in the subject.

CONTENTS

PART 1

The Employment relationship

PART 2

Termination of employment

Part 1

The Employment relationship

General questions and answers on key concepts of the employment relationship

1. EMPLOYMENT STATUS

Question

What is an employee?

Answer

All employees are workers as such, but an `employee'
has extra employment rights and responsibilities that
do not apply to workers who aren't employees.

These rights include all of those rights workers have
but additional rights such as:-

- Statutory Sick Pay
- Statutory maternity, paternity, adoption and shared
  parental leave and pay (workers only get pay, not
  leave)
- Minimum notice periods if their employment will be
  ending, for example if an employer is dismissing
  them
- Protection against unfair dismissal
- Right to request flexible working
- Time off for emergencies
- Statutory Redundancy Pay

https://www.gov.uk/employment-status/employee

Question

What is a worker?

Answer

A person is generally classed as a 'worker' if:

- they have a contract or other arrangement to do work or services personally for a reward (your contract doesn't have to be written)
- their reward is for money or a benefit in kind, for example the promise of a contract or future work
- they only have a limited right to send someone else to do the work (subcontract)
- they have to turn up for work even if they don't want to
- their employer has to have work for them to do as long as the contract or arrangement lasts
- they aren't doing the work as part of their own limited company in an arrangement where the 'employer' is actually a customer or client

https://www.gov.uk/employment-status/worker

Question

What rights do workers have?

Answer

Workers are entitled to certain employment rights, including:

- getting the National Minimum Wage
- protection against unlawful deductions from wages
- the statutory minimum level of paid holiday
- the statutory minimum length of rest breaks
- to not work more than 48 hours on average per week or to opt out of this right if they choose
- protection against unlawful discrimination
- protection for 'whistleblowing' - reporting wrongdoing in the workplace
- to not be treated less favourably if they work part-time

They may also be entitled to:

- Statutory Sick Pay
- Statutory Maternity Pay
- Statutory Paternity Pay
- Statutory Adoption Pay
- Shared Parental Pay

https://www.gov.uk/employment-status/worker

Question

What rights do workers not have?

Answer

Workers usually not entitled to:

- minimum notice periods if their employment will be ending, for example if an employer is dismissing them
- protection against unfair dismissal
- the right to request flexible working
- time off for emergencies
- Statutory Redundancy Pay

https://www.gov.uk/employment-status/worker

Question

Who are most likely to be classified as workers?

Answer

- People who occasionally do work for a specific business
- the business doesn't have to offer them work and they don't have to accept it - they only work when they want to
- their contract with the business uses terms like 'casual', 'freelance', 'zero hours', 'as required' or something similar
- they had to agree with the business's terms and conditions to get work - either verbally or in writing
- they are under the supervision or control of a manager or director
- they can't send someone else to do their work

- the business deducts tax and National Insurance contributions from their wages
- the business provides materials, tools or equipment they need to do the work

https://www.gov.uk/employment-status/worker

Question

What statute sets out the statutory definitions for `employee' and `worker' and what are they?

Suggested answer

The Employment Rights Act 1996 (ERA 96). S.230(1) defines an employee as `an individual who has entered into or works under (or, where the employment has cased, worked under) a contract of employment'. Under ERA 96 S.230(2) it states that a contract of employment `is a contract of service [employment] or apprenticeship, whether express or implied and (if it is express) whether oral or in writing`. More detail is provided in S.230 (3) defining a worker as an individual who has entered into, or works under, a contract of employment or `any other contract, whether express or implied and (if it is express) whether oral or in writing, whereby the individual undertakes to do or perform personally any work or services for another party to the contract whose status is not by virtue of the contract that of client or customer of any profession or business undertaking carried on by the individual'.

Question

Define what constitutes a worker under the Employment Rights Act 1996?

Suggested answer

A worker under the Employment Rights Act 1996 (ERA 96) is someone who works under either a contract of employment or any other contract under which the individual undertakes to work for the other party, except where the other party is a client of a business carried on by the individual (S.230(3) ERA 96.

Question

What is the distinction between a worker and an employee?

An employee is a person who works under a *contract of employment.* There are three tests for a person to satisfy employee status. An employee will be under an obligation to perform the contract *personally.* There must be what is known as a *mutuality of obligation* between the parties. Lastly, the employer must have a sufficient level of *control* over what the employee does. A worker will (or may) not be an employee if they are free to accept or reject offers of work made to them. A worker cannot claim unfair dismissal or a statutory redundancy payment. Workers have some statutory rights such as a right to be paid the National Minimum Wage (NMW), working hours and annual leave.

Question

What is meant by the term mutuality of obligations?

Suggested answer

This means if there is no obligation to provide work or obligation to accept work then no contract of employment exists between the parties and no employee status *(Carmichael v National Power PLC [1999])[ii]*.

Question

How have the courts and tribunals approached the issue of identifying employees?

Suggested answer

There is no statutory definition of a contract of service so the courts and tribunals have to apply their own criteria. The courts will give weight to the intentions of the parties or look at the contractual terms but may need to look at other factors. The common law **control test** gives the employer the right to tell the employee what to do, how, when, and where to do the job. Another key factor is whether there is a **mutuality of**

obligation between the employer and the individual. It is also vital in establishing employment status that the individual performs their service *in person.* In *Express and Echo Publications v Tanton [1999]*[iii] a contract allowed a worker to provide a substitute if he was not available to do the work. The Court of Appeal held that as there was no obligation for the worker to do the work personally he could not be an employee. In *MacFarlane v Glasgow City Council [2000]*[iv] gymnasts working in a local authority were able to provide substitutes for any shift they were unable to work. The substitutes were paid directly and the gymnasts could only be replaced by others on the council's approved list. *Tanton* was distinguished on this basis.

Question

What is an agency worker?

Suggested answer

An agency worker is someone who has a contract with an agency but works temporararily for the person/organisation who hires them. These agencies can be recruitment agencies for temporary staff. Agency workers do not include –

- Self employed people who may work through an agency but work for themselves who may be classified as `self employed instead'

- Those using an agency to find either permanent or fixed term employment

Question

Can a contract of employment exist between an agency and a person working through an agency?

Suggested answer

It depends. In *Dacas v Brooke Street Bureau [2004]* [v]Dacas was held <u>not</u> to be an employee of the agency for the purposes of unfair dismissal. There was no implied contract between the claimant and end-user of the services (as there was no express contract between them), so unless they could argue they were employed by the agency they could not make a claim for unfair dismissal.

In contrast to this is *Cairns v Visteon Ltd [2007]*[vi] a contract of employment was held to exist and the EAT did not feel it was necessary to imply a contract with the end-user.

In *James v London Borough of Greenwich [2008]* [vii], the Court of Appeal upheld a tribunal decision that an agency worker was not employed by the end-user to which she had been supplied by an employment agency. In doing so it held that whether an agency worker is employed by an end-user must be decided in accordance with common law principles of implied contract and, in some very extreme cases, by exposing sham arrangements. Just as it is wrong to consider all agency workers to be outside the protection of the Employment Rights Act 1996 (ERA 1996), and therefore unable to claim unfair dismissal, it is not possible for all agency workers to argue successfully that they are employees.

https://uk.practicallaw.thomsonreuters.com

Question

What are the Agency Workers Regulation 2010?

Suggested answer

These are based on EU law and introduced the principle of equal treatment for agency workers after they have been on the `same role' for the same hirer for a qualifying period of 12 calendar weeks. Agency workers now have the right under Regulation 5 to the same `basic working and employment conditions' as if they would have been entitled to if they had been directly engaged by the hirer.

Question

What are zero hours contracts?

Answer

These are contracts where an employer is under no obligation to offer work and the person who works under them is under no obligation to accept any work offered to them.

Question

What is the `gig economy'?

Answer

Around 1.3 million now work in the gig economy. It is a form of self-employment with those working under these arrangements having few rights. Work can be delivered via a platform on the internet or even an app. Companies like Uber and Deliveroo have become well known as being involved in this type of employment.

Question

What are some key recent case decisions involving `gig economy' cases?

Answer

In *Uber BV v Aslam [2018]*[viii] the Court of Appeal upholding the EAT decision held that drivers should have worker status. Uber had argued that it only acted as an *intermediary,* providing booking and payment services, and the drivers drive the passengers as *independent contractors.* This was covered in their written terms. The drivers argued Uber contracts with the passengers to provide driving services, which the drivers perform for it. The majority in the Court of Appeal held that these terms do not reflect the practical reality of the relationship and can be ignored. The court relied upon the decision in *Autoclenz Ltd v Belcher [2011]* [ix] where a court can disregard the terms of any contract created by the employer in as far as it seeks to characterise the relationship between the employer and the individuals who provide the services (whether they are employees or workers) in a particular artificial way.

In *Pimlico Plumbers Ltd v Smith [2018]* [x] Mr Smith worked as a plumber for Pimlico Plumbers for six years until 2011. He successfully argued in the Employment Tribunal then the Employment Appeal Tribunal and then the Court of Appeal that he was a worker for the purposes of employment legislation. Pimlico maintained that he was a 'self-employed operative' – which is how he was described in the agreement between Mr Smith and Pimlico - and appealed to the Supreme Court.

Despite the fact that Mr Smith filed tax returns on the basis that he was self-employed, was VAT registered, was entitled to reject work and was able to take outside work, the Supreme Court held that the Employment Tribunal had been entitled to find that he was a 'worker'. Significant factors in its decision included:

- Mr Smith was required to wear a Pimlico branded uniform and to use a Pimlico branded van leased from Pimlico.

- Mr Smith had to carry a Pimlico identity card and closely follow the administrative instructions of its control room.

- The contract referred to 'wages', 'gross misconduct' and 'dismissal', and included a suite of restrictive covenants concerning Mr Smith's working activities following termination.

- While Mr Smith was able to swap assignments with other plumbers already working for Pimlico, this was more akin to swapping a shift between workers than providing a substitute – this was not a case where the employer was uninterested in the identity of the substitute.

2. THE CONTRACT OF EMPLOYMENT

Question

What is a contract of employment?

Suggested answer

Contracts of employment are a specialised form of contract that are subject to the general principles of contract law. Some contracts are negotiated individually but in workplaces where unions are recognised may also be subject to collective agreements as well as `works rules' or other guidance.

Question

What terms are likely to be in employment contracts?

Suggested answer

Examples of terms a contract of employment could include are job title and description of role and work, rates of pay, holiday entitlements and other leave including sick leave and pay arrangements, working hours, pension arrangements, type of contract (fixed term, temporary, part time etc) location of job and any mobility clauses. The contract is unlikely to contain all the details of employment but instead refer to other sources containing rules and guidance dealing with more issues (i.e. disciplinary, grievance procedures etc).

Question

What is a `written statement'?

Suggested answer

A written statement must be provided with the particulars of the key terms of their employment under S.1 and S.2 of the ERA 96. This must be given to a person not later than <u>2 months</u> after they start their employment where their employment will continue for a month or more. This is referred to as a *written statement* or a S.1 statement. Ideally this should be given to the individual but S.2(2) and S.2 (3) enable a selection of the key terms may be made *reasonably accessible* to them in a document they are referred to.

Question

What are key terms in a written (or S.1) statement?

Suggested answer

The following key information must be included in a single document which is known as the "principal statement".

- Name of employer and employee.

- Date employment and continuous employment started.

- Job location.

- Pay and whether it's weekly, monthly etc.

- Working hours.

- Holiday entitlement.

- Job description / job title.

- Details of any collective agreement that directly affect the employee's conditions of employment.

Employers may provide other documents such and staff handbooks, or staff intranet sites for the following information :

- sick leave and pay entitlement

- pensions and pension schemes

- disciplinary and grievance procedures

- appeals procedure under the disciplinary and grievance procedures.

Advice from ACAS where you have not received this information in the way described above is: -

If an employee does not receive a written statement they should try to resolve the matter informally in the first instance, however, if this doesn't work they should raise a formal grievance. As a last resort employees could make a claim to an employment tribunal, where the tribunal could award compensation, which could be 2 - 4 week's pay. www.acas.org.uk

Question

Are there any likely changes coming to S.1 statements?

Suggested answer

Yes. There are some changes due to take place amending the Section 1 requirements on providing written statements. The regulations are:-

- The Employment Rights (Miscellaneous Amendments) Regulations 2019
- The Employment Rights (Employment Particulars and Paid Annual Leave) (Amendment) Regulations 2018

These regulations are effective from 6 April 2020. Some of the key provisions are:-

- Converts "employee" to "worker" which means that "workers" as well as "employees" have the right to a section 1 statement.
- There will be a right to be given a statement from day one of starting work. There is no longer an exception for jobs lasting less than one month.
- There are additional requirements for the section 1 statement and note that these must be contained in a single document (not instalments). These additional particulars are:

  - ✓ Information confirming the days of the week the worker is required to work and whether working hours or days may be variable, with details of how they may vary.
  - ✓ Confirm entitlement to paid leave, including maternity leave and paternity leave.
  - ✓ Any other remuneration or benefits provided by the employer.
  - ✓ Any probationary period, including any conditions and its duration.

- ✓ Any training provided by the employer which the worker is required to complete and any other required training in respect of which the employer will not bear the cost.

Other particulars currently included in a supplementary statement will have to be given in the <u>principal statement</u>. These are:-

- ✓ The notice periods for termination by either side.
- ✓ Terms relating to absence due to incapacity and sick pay.
- ✓ Terms as to length of temporary or fixed-term work.
- ✓ Terms related to work outside the UK for a period of more than one month.

Although not part of the changes to Section 1 statement, The Employment Rights (Employment Particulars and Paid Annual Leave) (Amendment) Regulations 2018 makes an important change to reference periods in relation to paid annual leave. These regulations amend regulation 16 of the <u>Working Time Regulations 1998</u> to increase the reference period for determining an average week's pay (for the purposes of calculating holiday pay where variable remuneration or no normal working hours) from 12 weeks to 52 weeks, or the number of complete weeks for which the worker has been employed.

Question

What are collective agreements and work's rules?

Suggested answer

Collective agreements are those negotiated between the employer and a recognised union on behalf of staff (members and non-members benefit for the terms negotiated). They may or may not be legally enforceable depending on whether the terms and conditions have been **incorporated** into individual employment contracts through express provision to this effect. They can be expressly incorporated in S.1 ERA 96 written statements of particulars or through custom and practice, or even implied by conduct of employee happy to work under the terms of a collective agreement.

Works rules are terms usually created unilaterally and enforced by the employer. These may be incorporated expressly or impliedly into the employee's individual contract of employment. Examples are disciplinary rules and procedure and grievance procedures etc.

Question

What are the implied terms?

Suggested answer

Terms can be implied by statute or common law. The National Minimum Wage Act 1998 (NMWA 1998) is one example of where minimum rates of pay have been set by the government and must be complied with in employment contracts. Two examples of statutory implied terms. The Working Time Regulations 1998 (WTR 1998) deals with minimum holiday periods and maximum hours (noting certain occupation exemptions). Terms can be implied by law through court decisions such as the old *Moorcock [1889]* [xi]test of giving `business efficacy' to the employment relationship. Or where a term should be blatantly obvious that the party relying on an implied term thought it unnecessary to agree an express term using the `officious bystander' objective test.

Question

What are the duties of the employer?

Suggested answer

- To pay wages
- Provide work
- Cooperate with the employee
- Take reasonable care of the employee

Question

What obligations do employers have to pay wages?

Suggested answer

This is usually an express term in the employment contract where there is an amount agreed. It is important to point out that an employer has to comply with the National Minimum Wage and National Living Wage. The current rates are –

YEAR	25 and over	21 - 24	18- 20	Under 18	Apprentice
2019	£8.21	£7.70	£6.15	£4.35	£3.90

Providing workers are ready and willing to perform their contracts but due to sickness or unavoidable impediment will be entitled to their wages *(Burns v Santander PLC [2011][xii].)*

Question

What obligations do employers have to provide work?

Suggested answer

This may be a more limited obligation. It is not seen as a general obligation for an employer to actually provide work for employees, but in some cases a failure to do this could be a breach of contract. An employee paid commission for work performed could suffer a pay detriment if work not provided. A professional employee may need to keep updating their skills and knowledge and lack of work could have a negative affect on continuing development and reputation.

Question

What is meant by the duty to cooperate with the employee?

Suggested answer

Both the employer and employee have what is known as a `duty of trust and confidence'. An employer should not breach this duty in terms of their obligations. In *Malik v BCCI [1997]* [xiii]the House of Lords confirmed that employers must not destroy the mutual trust and confidence upon which *cooperation* is built upon without a reasonable and proper cause.

Some examples: -

Reprimanding an employee in public or before colleagues. (*Morrow v Safeway Stores plc [2002])*[xiv].

No disciplinary policy followed giving employee chance to defend himself (*Hilton v Shiner Builders Merchants [2001])*[xv].

Not being offered enhanced redundancy terms offered to other employees. (*BG Plc v O'Brien [2001]*) [xvi]

The employer operating a business in a dishonest and corrupt manner which damaged an innocent employee's reputation (*Malik* above).

The employer using their discretion under a mobility clause making it impossible for an employee to comply with a contractual obligation to move *(United Bank Ltd v Akhtar [1989])*[xvii].

Other examples could be false allegations of theft without evidence or failing to make reasonable adjustments.

Question

What is the duty owed by the employer to take reasonable care of their employee/s?

Suggested answer

The employer has a number of legal duties owed to an employee which are both based on obligations imposed by common law and statute.

There is a common law duty of care which imposes an implied term into a contract of employment to take reasonable care to ensure the safety of employees. This normally falls within the tort of negligence and the duty of care/standard of care owed to employees. This was described in case law as the standard of care `an ordinary prudent employer would take in all circumstances' *(Paris v Stepney Borough Council [1951]*[xviii]*)*. There is a need for safe premises of work

31

(Latimer v AEC Ltd [1953][xix]*)* as well as a safe system of work (i.e. protective clothing, training and supervision – *Walker v Northumberland County Council [1995]*[xx] *& Wilson & Clyde Coal Co Ltd v English [1938]*[xxi]*)* Bullying and harassment has also been found to come under the remit of the employer providing a safe system of work *(Barber v Somerset County Council: [2004]*[xxii]*)*.

The employer has a number of statutory duties to comply with and incorporated into contracts of employment as implied terms. Section 2(2) of <u>Health and Safety at Work Act (HSWA) 1974</u> requires employer's to provide training, instruction and information in sufficient detail to enable the employee to understand the hazards they face. In addition the <u>Management of Health and Safety at Work Regulations 1992</u> (MHSWR) require employers to carry out workplace assessments on all operations and processes that could raise a potential risk to the health and safety of employees. The employer has other duties under the HSWA 1974. There is a general rule covering all types of employment under S.2(1):-

"It shall be the duty of every employer, to ensure, so far as reasonably practicable, the health, safety and welfare of all his employees"

There is more detail within the Act under Section 2 adding more detail on the obligations required to promote a safe system of work without risk to health, noting reasonably practicable proviso.

Health and safety protection has been extended by subsequent legislation (mainly related to EU Directives) such as The Manual Handling Operations Regulations 1992 , The supply of machinery (Safety) Regulations 1992 (Machinery Regulations) and The Workplace (Health, Safety and Welfare) Regulations 1992.

On the issue of references, the employer has no general duty to provide references but if one is provided, there may be a claim under the tort of negligent misstatement if economic loss results. There may also be a claim under discrimination if the employer only provides references for white or non-disabled employees. An employer must take reasonable care when compiling a reference and that the information is accurate *(Spring v Guardian Assurance plc [1994]xxiii)*. The person providing a reference must not give an impression that is unfair or misleading overall, even if various parts of the reference are accurate. The issue of fairness in a reference and the impression it gives has been held to go beyond just the basic facts *(Jackson v Liverpool City Council [2011]xxiv)*.

Question

What are the duties of the employee?

Suggested answer

- To cooperate with the employer

- To take reasonable care and indemnify
- Duty of Fidelity or good faith

Question

What is meant by the duty to cooperate with the employer?

Suggested answer

This would cover a duty of an employee to obey reasonable orders or instructions and not wilfully disobey `lawful' orders *(Laws v London Chronicle Ltd [1959]*[xxv]*)*. A work-to-rule has amounted to a breach of contract if seen as designed to disrupt work *(Secretary of State for Employment v ASLEF (No 2) [1972]*[xxvi]*)*.

Question

What does the duty of reasonable care and indemnify involve?

Suggested answer

The employee is under a duty to exercise reasonable care and skill in the way he/she performs their duties. If he/she performs their duties negligently or incompetently they will be in breach of this duty and liable to indemnify their employer for any losses they have suffered as a result of the breach *(Lister v Romford Ice and Cold Storage Co Ltd [1957]*[xxvii]*)*. Also there is a statutory obligation under S.7 of the HSWA 1974 that employees take reasonable care of themselves and other work colleagues who may be affected by their acts and omissions in the workplace.

Question

What is the Duty of Fidelity or good faith?

Suggested answer

This duty covers a number of elements of confidentiality and non-competition. A case involving confidentiality was *Crowson Fabrics Ltd v Rider and Others [2007]*[xxviii]. Employees who had copied customer contact details and sales figures during employment were held not to have acted in breach of their implied duty of confidentiality. This was because the information was not confidential as it was in the public domain. They were however, held to have breached their duty of fidelity.

An employee was held to have breached his contract and fiduciary duties when he helped set up a business that would compete with his employer's business whilst he was on `garden leave' *(Imam-Sadeque v Blue Bay Asset Management (Services) Ltd [2012]*[xxix]).

Where an employee works for a competitor outside their working hours this may not necessarily be a breach of the employees duty of fidelity. It depends how harmful the other employment is to the employer's business. In *Hivac Ltd v Park Royal Scientific Instruments Ltd [1946]*[xxx] a handful of skilled workers who assembled hearing aids worked for their employer's competitor on Sundays. The Court of Appeal held they were in breach of he implied duty of fidelity because this was not seen as consistent with their contract of employment to do work in their spare time that could potentially cause harm to their employers.

Once an employee ends their employment they can compete as an ex-employee with their former employer without any restrictions. Any restrictive covenant attempting to restrict competition such as above, will be subject to the doctrine of restraint of trade.

Question

Is there an obligation not to compete with the employer?

Suggested answer

Unless there is an express term in the contract prohibiting working outside working hours, it will not necessarily be a breach of the employee's duty of fidelity where the employee works for a competitor. The issue will be what damage this outside employment has on the employer's business.

In *Hivac Ltd v Park Royal Scientific Instruments Ltd [1946]* (discussed above) 5 skilled manual workers who assembled hearing aids worked for their employer's only competitor on Sundays. They were held by the Court of Appeal to be in breach of the implied duty of fidelity as it was not seen as consistent with their contract of employment working in their spare time something that has potential of being harmful to their employer. The fact they worked for their only competitor played a part in the way this decision was made.

In order for the employee's duty of fidelity to be breached, he/she would usually have access to confidential information or trade secrets with the danger that information ending up in a competitor's hands.

At the end of an employee's employment he/she may compete with his previous employer without restriction (restrictive covenants attempting to restrict competition are subject to the doctrine of restraint of trade).

Question

What is a conflict of interest and duty?

Suggested answer

This relates to a conflict between employee's duty of fidelity to his employer and his personal interest. It can involve an employee about to leave his employment and set up in competition wanting to get information from his employer or entice away his employer's customers and staff. In *Roger Bullivant Ltd v Ellis [1987]*[xxxi] it was held a breach of the employee's duty of fidelity to make lists of existing customers with the intention of using it after the end of his employment. This also included deliberately memorizing a list for such purposes *(Robb v Green [1895]xxxii)*. Also a breach of duty to entice away or agree to work personally for existing customers of the employer or induce other employees to break their contracts of employment *(Sanders v Parry [1967]xxxiii)*.

Question

What about trade secrets and confidential information?

Suggested answer

Where an employee during his/her employment uses or reveals trade secrets or other information of a confidential nature, or it has been impressed on the employee as being confidential, he/she will be in breach of their duty of fidelity *(Faccenda Chicken Ltd v Fowler [1986xxxiv])*. Lists of customers are likely to be confidential or information relating to trade secrets or even working methods. Information of a trivial nature or mundane kind, or information from the public domain will not be seen as confidential information, even if an express term in the contract.

After the employee's employment has ended the employee is only prohibited from revealing or using his previous employer's trade secrets or highly confidential equivalent to a trade secret (*Faccenda* case).

Part 2

Termination of employment

A mix of general and problem questions and answers on unfair dismissal, wrongful dismissal and constructive dismissal claims

Question

What is unfair dismissal?

Suggested answer

All employees in the UK have the right not to be dismissed unfairly. Section 94(1) <u>ERA 96</u> states that *'an employee has the right not to be unfairly dismissed by his employer'.* The employer must have acted reasonably in dismissing an employee and this usually means have followed a fair process leading up to the dismissal. The person claiming unfair dismissal must be an "employee" not a "worker" or self-employed person for instance. Certain reasons for dismissal will come under the umbrella of `automatically unfair dismissal'. These include:-

- Asserting your statutory rights;
- Trade union membership or activities (or non-union membership;
- Exercising rights in relation to the statutory recognition of a trade union;
- Pregnancy or maternity;
- Certain health and safety grounds;
- Refusing to comply with a requirement which is in contravention of the <u>Working Time Regulations 1998</u> (WTR);
- The reason, or the principle reason for the dismissal, is that the employee made a protected disclosure;

- The employee is dismissed for trying to enforce the National Minimum Wage or National Living Wage;
- The dismissal of a `worker` within 12 weeks of taking part in protected industrial action;
- The exercise of a statutory right to request a contract variation;
- The exercise of rights under the Part-time Workers (Prevention of Less Favourable Treatment) Regulations 2000 and the Fixed-term Employees (Prevention of Less Favourable Treatment) Regulations) 2002;
- The exercise of a right relating to study leave or training;
- Political opinions or affiliations (S.13 Enterprise and Regulatory Reform Act 2013)

Question

What is the relevance of procedural fairness?

Suggested answer

The Employment Act 2002 introduced a statutory dismissal and disciplinary procedure and a statutory grievance procedure. Section 98A(1) ERA 96 provides that an employee who is dismissed without the relevant statutory procedure being completed will be regarded as unfairly dismissed if this was wholly or mainly because of the employer's failure to comply with its requirements.

The employment tribunal has to apply the statutory test of fairness as set out Section 98 (4) of the ERA 1996. This provides:

"the determination of the question whether the dismissal is fair or unfair (having regard to the reason shown by the employer) –

(a) depends on whether in the circumstances (including the size and administration resources of the employer's undertaking) the employer acted reasonably or unreasonably in treating it as a sufficient reason for dismissing the employee; and

(b) that question shall be determined in accordance with equity and the substantial merits of the case."

Paragraph 4 of the ACAS Code of Practice on Disciplinary and Grievance Procedures 2015 sets out a number of elements to fairness. These are:-

- o Employers and employees should raise and deal with issues promptly and should not unreasonably delay meetings, decisions, or confirmation of these decisions;
- o Employers and employees should act in a consistent way;
- o Important that employers carry out the necessary investigations to establish the facts of the case;
- o Employers should let employees know the basis of the issue or problem and give the employee the chance to put their case in response, before any decisions are made *(Spence v Department*

of Agriculture and Rural Development [2011][xxxv];

- o Employers should allow employees the opportunity to be accompanied at any formal disciplinary or grievance meeting; and
- o Employers should give the employee the chance to appeal against any formal decision made.

The importance of following the Code is that failure to do so could result in an upward or downward adjustment to any award of 25% depending on if the employer or employee failed to comply with the code.

Question

Are there `fair` reasons for dismissal?

Suggested answer

Yes an employer can dismiss an employee for potentially fair reasons. These should fall within one of the following categories (S. 98 ERA 96) –

- ✓ It relates to the **capacity** (includes health reasons) or qualifications of the employee;
- ✓ It relates to the **conduct** of the employee;
- ✓ The employee was made **redundant**;
- ✓ The employee could not continue to work in the position held without contravention, either on the employer's or employee's part, or a duty or **restriction imposed by or under a statute**;

- ✓ There was **some other substantial reason** to justify the dismissal of an employee holding the position that the employer held.

1. Capability or qualifications

This is set out in S.98 (3) <u>ERA 96.</u> The term `capability' relates to `*skill, aptitude, health or any other physical or mental quality'.* The reference to `qualifications' means `*any degree, diploma, or other academic, technical or professional qualification relevant to the position which the employee held'.*

2. Conduct

Certain behaviour may come under the umbrella of conduct which reflects badly on the nature of the employment relationship and be a reason ultimately for a dismissal to be considered fair. The employer must have followed a fair process through its disciplinary procedures to avoid it being unfair. Thus the employer must have acted reasonably in dismissing the employee.

Some areas:-

- Continually missing work
- Poor discipline
- Drug or alcohol abuse
- Theft or dishonesty

A key case is *British Home Stores v Burchell [1978]* [xxxvi] where a test known later as the "Burchell test" was established. In this case the judge said that what the employment tribunal had to decide was not whether the employee was *actually guilty of misconduct or not*, but instead was:-

1. Whether the employer actually believed that the employee was guilty of misconduct,

2. Whether it had reasonable grounds on which to base that belief, and

3. Whether it had carried out as much investigation as was reasonable in the circumstances of the particular case.

3. The employee is being made redundant

This is dealt with in detail in the third volume of my series but basically this could potentially be unfair selection for redundancy compared with other colleagues for instance.

4. Statutory ban

This is a potentially fair reason for dismissal in situations where an Employer has to dismiss an Employee because they are not able to continue in that job without contravening some law (S.98(2)(d) ERA 96). An example is an employee employed to drive a vehicle who has been banned due to a driving offence under road traffic laws.

5. Some other substantive reason

Section 98(1)(b) <u>ERA 96</u> gives tribunals the discretion to accept as a fair reason for dismissal something that does not fit conveniently into any other categories. This can situations where a member of staff is considered to be causing dissention amongst other employees *GM Gorfin v Distressed Gentlefolks Aid Association* [1973] [xxxvii]. In this case her dismissal by the manager was considered fair dismissal in order to restore harmony amongst the staff.

In *Foot v Eastern Counties Timber Co Ltd* [1972][xxxviii] Mrs Foot's husband commenced an electrical business that was believed by her employer to be in competition with their own. She was therefore dismissed from her employment as a wages and accounts clerk. The tribunal held that her employer's actions were reasonable due to the confidential nature of the information she had access to as her husband's company would be in competition with her employer.

In *Alboni (Respondent) v Ind Coope Retail Ltd (Appellants)* [1998][xxxix] the Court of Appeal held that where a husband and wife had a joint contract of employment managing a public house and that it was expressly provided that termination of one partner would automatically terminate the other partner's contract, this came under other substantial reason. This was decided before the <u>Equality Act 2010</u> which may have resulted in a different outcome.

Barnes v Gilmartin Association [1998]^{xl}, was a case where a part-time employee was required to work full time. There was no redundancy as there was no diminution in the employer requiring the employee to carry out work of a particular kind. The dismissal therefore fell under the category of some other substantial reason as a result of business re-organisation.

The employer does not have to show that a reorganisation or rearrangement of working patterns or the change of contractual terms were essential. In *Hollister v National Farmers Union [1979]^{xli}* the Court of Appeal held that a "sound, good business reason" was sufficient to establish the criteria for some other substantial reason for dismissing the employee, who refused to accept a change in his terms and conditions of employment.

Question

What is the form needed to issue a claim?

Suggested answer

A claimant needs to complete a claim form known as an **ET1**. This can be submitted on line (most common method now), or by post or in person. Claimants must use the ET1 (it is compulsory) and if a claim is submitted on the wrong form or unreadable it will be rejected. Two or more claimants can submit a group claim using the same form if their claims are *"based on* the same set of facts" (<u>Rule 9 Employment Tribunal Rules 2013</u>). The ACAS EC Certificate reference number must be entered on the ET1 form or it will be rejected. In *Sterling v United Learning Trust [2015]*[xlii] a form was rejected as all of the numbers were not written correctly. The ET1 must be submitted to the employment tribunal within three months (less one day) of the effective date of termination (EDT).

Question

What form is used to respond to a claim?

Suggested answer

The ET1 is sent to the tribunal and if the form is not rejected, a copy is sent to the employer who will need to complete their response on an **ET3** form where the employer sets out his/her response to the ET1 claim. A copy also goes to ACAS. The ET3 response form must be completed and sent back *within 28 days of the date that the tribunal office sends the employer the copy of the claim.*

Question

How does ACAS Early Conciliation work?

Suggested answer

Before submitting a claim to the employment tribunal, in most cases the individual must first inform ACAS of the complaint in order to explore use of conciliation avoiding the need for litigation. This is called early conciliation (EC) and is governed by the Early Conciliation Rules of Procedure contained within the Schedule to the <u>Employment Tribunals (Early Conciliation: Exemptions and Rules of Procedure) Regulations 2014</u>. The service is mandatory and free.

There are some exemptions to the EC under Rule 3 of the EC Rules of Procedure. These are:-

- ✓ Where it is a joint claim and another person has already begun EC relating to the same dispute;
- ✓ The claim is included with another claim to which EC does not apply;
- ✓ The claim is for interim relief; or
- ✓ The claim is against the Security Service, the Secret Intelligence Service or the Government Communications Headquarters.

There is no obligation to actually engage in settlement discussions which is voluntary for both sides.

<u>How does EC work?</u>

ACAS EC is initiated by a potential claimant completing an ACAS EC Notification Form available from their website. The potential claimant must submit the Form to ACAS normally within the three months (less one day) to enter a claim. Basic contact details are requested on the Form mainly to identify the employer. In the case of more than one respondent, an EC Notification Form must be completed by each respondent and submitted within the three month period.

Once the Form has been received:-

- o ACAS promises to make first contact by telephone with a prospective claimant *within one working day*, and if the claimant agrees allocate them a named conciliator who will try and resolve the dispute through telephone calls to each side;

- o ACAS then has *four weeks* to try to achieve a settlement through the EC procedure. This period can be extended by the conciliator by another *two weeks* if it is thought there is a reasonable prospect of a settlement and both parties agree to this;

- o If it is possible for the parties to reach a final settlement, ACAS will record this as a *COT3 Settlement Agreement;*

- o If no settlement can be agreed at the end of the EC period, ACAS will issue the potential claimant with an ACAS EC Certificate to show that conciliation was considered. The certificate will have a reference number that the claimant must have to issue his/her claim

In terms of the three month period to submit a claim the "clock is stopped" will the parties take part in EC and restart at the end of the process.

Question

What are the important time limits?

Suggested answer

In most cases the time limit for bringing a claim is within three months (less one day) from the act complained of. For instance a claim for unfair dismissal a person dismissed on 20 June, the claim would have to be issued on or before 19 September. Section 111 of the ERA 96 titled *"Complaints to employment tribunal"* says that the claim must be brought *"before the end of the period of three months beginning with the effective date of termination"*. There are exceptions for certain types of claim which allow for a longer time limit of *six months*. This is the case in equal pay claims; unfair dismissal during industrial action and for statutory redundancy payments.

The tribunal has limited powers to grant an extension of time in certain claims. This will be either where:-

- It was not reasonably practicable to issue the claim in time, and it was issued within such further time as was reasonable; or
- It was "just and equitable" to extend time.

Extensions of time are rare so advisable to stick to the set time limits to avoid claim being rejected.

Question

What is meant by Initial Consideration?

Suggested answer

This is the next stage after the ET1 Claim Form and ET3 Response form have been received and accepted as correctly completed and submitted. The next stage is called Initial Consideration (also known as the "sift) where these documents are checked over by an employment judge. If the judge thinks either the Claim or the Response is unlikely to succeed they must notify that party, and instruct them to come and explain at a preliminary hearing why the claim should progress to a full hearing, rather than being struck out.

Problem question scenario

Unfair dismissal 1 – Before submitting a claim

Sayed is a member of staff working at Woodstones Tours Ltd as a tour operator. Woodstones is a medium sized London based company arranging tours around London. He had worked for the company over three years.

John was Sayed's direct line manager. Sayed raised some concerns about the increased number of hours he had been working without extra pay. John said he would look into it. A few days later Sayed received a letter informing him he was no longer required due to downturn in work and was being dismissed after working his notice period.

He has come to you to offer him help and advice with a view to possibly raising a claim against the company possibly for unfair dismissal but does not know how to go about this. Can you advise him if he has a case for unfair dismissal?

Suggested answer plan

Initial requirements

The first thing you would need to determine is whether Sayed meets all the criteria to bring a claim against Woodstones Tours Ltd for an unfair dismissal claim.

In order for Sayed to bring a claim for unfair dismissal he needs to establish he is an `employee'. The ERA 1996 (ERA 96) S.230(1) defines an employee as `an individual who has entered into or works under (or, where the employment has cased, worked under) a contract of employment'. Under ERA 96 S.230(2) it states that a contract of employment `is a contract of service [employment] or apprenticeship, whether express or implied and (if it is express) whether oral or in writing`. The first key issue then is to establish that

Sayed is an employee as opposed to say self-employed or a `worker' even. If he is able to show you his contract of employment this would be an important document that may state his employment status. If there is no contract of employment then other factors may come into play to determine Sayed's employment status such as the tests the courts can use discussed above (Control test, need for personal service, mutuality of obligations) to confirm employment status.

Another crucial factor is the need for sufficient qualifying employment. It appears he has worked for Woodstones Tours for three years so seems to meet the requirement that the employee has worked for their employer for at least two years to bring a claim (S.108 ERA 96). It is important Sayed is also advised to be aware of the strict time limits for bringing a claim (three months less one day).

The claim

After you have confirmed Sayed's employment status, qualifying service and checked it is within the strict time limits for bringing a claim, then the substance of the claim can be determined. One the face of it, it would appear Sayed has been dismissed from his job without any recourse to disciplinary or grievance procedures. An employer should have processes it follows which enable an employer to go through a fair procedure which enables the employee the chance to know what action they may face and the opportunity to defend themselves (and be represented). This is governed by ACAS codes of practice and guidance requiring employers to have sufficient rules and regulations in place to protect employees from arbitrary unfair treatment without recourse to redress. The fact that Sayed has been dismissed out of hand without a fair reason as defined under S.98 ERA 96 (i.e. lack of capacity or qualifications for the job, conduct of the employee, being made redundant or other substantive reason) appears to give him a cause of action for unfair dismissal. Once you are happy you have established the initial requirements are met then you can inform Sayed you are happy to advise him on his case and the various procedures he to be undergone. It is useful at this stage to request any documents he may have in his possession to assist in the conduct of the case, especially company guidance, relevant correspondence and remuneration information on wages/pension etc useful for a claim.

Problem question scenario

Unfair dismissal 2 - The ACAS Early Conciliation procedure

You are a trainee solicitor/paralegal and Mary is a client of your firm Brown Solicitors. You are helping her prepare her unfair dismissal claim against her previous employer, Star Reprographics Ltd. She is very keen to understand more about the how the ACAS Early Conciliation procedure actually works. Mary is concerned she will be forced to settle her claim for unfair dismissal on unfair terms (in her view) and wants her `day in court' to get what she feels she deserves.

Can you advise Mary on the ACAS Early Conciliation Procedure?

Suggested answer plan

Mary should be advised that the ACAS Early Conciliation procedure (EC) is a mandatory stage of the procedure and has to used *before* a claim is submitted. The EC offers the chance for the parties to try to resolve their differences through the EC process and maybe avoid the need to progress with actual litigation. This is a "pre claim" process. The Early Conciliation Rules of Procedure are found in the *Schedule to the Employment Tribunals (Early Conciliation: Exemptions and Rules of Procedure) Regulations 2014*. The service is free so Mary will not have to contribute any money towards it.

The important point to make Mary aware of is she is under no obligation to take part in settlement discussions. The aim of the procedure is to inform ACAS of the potential claim so they are able to present the chance of conciliation at the early stage.

The ACAS EC is started by the potential claimant completing an ACAS EC Notification Form found on their website at: https://ec.acas.org.uk/. Mary needs to be aware of time limits to comply with. As potential claimant she must submit the EC Notification Form within three months (the normal time limit for bringing a claim) which can be submitted on-line or through the post. The Form itself only asks for basic details including names and contact details of all the parties. The aim at this stage is to identify and contact the employer. The form does not ask for information about the dispute itself. It may be helpful to also explain to Mary what happens after the Form has been received. The various stages are:

- ACAS promises to make first contact via telephone with a prospective claimant within *one working day*, and with their agreement allocate a named councillor to them whose job will be to try to resolve the dispute through exchange of telephone calls to each side of the dispute;
- ACAS has *four weeks* to try to achieve a settlement through EC. This period can be extended by a further *two weeks* if there is a reasonable prospect of a settlement and both parties agree;
- If in this case Mary reaches a settlement with Star Reprographics Ltd then a COT3 Settlement Agreement is recorded; and
- Where in this case Mary and Star Reprographics are unable to reach a settlement, ACAS will issue Mary as the potential claimant with an ACAS EC certificate to show that conciliation was considered. This certificate has

a reference number and the claimant will not be able to issue a claim without this number.

It is important for Mary to know that after a claim has been issued ACAS has a statutory duty to continue with conciliation to help the parties to settle their dispute, right up until the claim draws to an end.

It is important to reassure Mary that the period involved in EC has the effect of "stopping the clock" during the three month time limit until ACAS gives the EC Certificate to the claimant.

In summary it is important to reassure Mary that the Early Conciliation procedure is a compulsory part of the process leading up to submitting a claim so she has to comply with this requirement. It is not meant to pressurize claimants (or respondents) into settlement discussions or pursuing a claim. It is a chance to explore if there is some common ground or compromise that can be made to avoid litigation which can be time consuming, traumatic and stressful for the parties. The advice to Mary is to engage in the process of EC, prepare well and accept it is a necessary procedure to adhere to pre-claim.

Question

What is wrongful dismissal?

Suggested answer

A wrongful dismissal is a dismissal without notice or not

with adequate notice in situations where proper notice should have been given. A wrongful dismissal claim is for a breach of contract and can be brought by any employee, and only requires *one month employment.* Notice is required but depends mainly on how long an employee has worked. After one month it is a week's notice, after two years, it is one week's notice for each complete year to a maximum of twelve weeks on and after twelve years. It involves a breach of contract so is based on contractual obligations of the employer. No length of service is required for a breach of contract claim. A claim for wrongful dismissal can be brought in the county court or the High Court If the claim arises out of or is outstanding after termination of employment and its value does not exceed £25,000 then it can be brought to an employment tribunal.

The damages that can be awarded normally equate to the value of the employee's pay and benefits during the period of notice that the employee would have been given, had the contract been terminated lawfully.

It differs from unfair dismissal as it is a contractual right rather than a statutory one.

Problem question scenario

Wrongful dismissal – Claim for wrongful dismissal scenario

Mario comes to you as a legal advisor specializing in employment law to offer him advice or guidance on his situation.

Up until recently he worked in a well known established university as a researcher in laboratory researching genetic profiling. A week ago he got into an argument with his manager John Saltly, the Project Lead over standard of work and he dismissed him summarily without notice quoting his poor standard of work and gross misconduct for arguing aggressively with his manager. He was dismissed with no Payment in Lieu of Notice (PILON) stating he could do this under the company handbook. Mario shows you his contract of employment which shows he is entitled to six month's notice with an option of PILON. He wants to know what his rights are and if he has a claim. Mario also insists his work has always been completed to a high standard with no previous criticism of his competency or performance of his work. Can you advise Mario?

The first important thing to do when contacted by Mario is to ask him to bring in all the relevant documents that will assist you in offering him guidance or advice. Key documents would be the contract of employment in order to check the relevant clauses, particularly in this case the clause referring to the six month notice period. Any other documentation he has relating to any company disciplinary procedures, and his pay statements and other relevant documents concerning any disciplinary action taking against him, in this case around competency or performance.

If after checking the contract, it clearly indicates that

Mario is entitled to six month's notice either worked or paid in lieu of notice. You can inform him that on the face of it he should be entitled to be paid for his contractual notice, i.e. six month's pay (and any other contractual benefits he may be entitled to which should form part of your discussion with him). The basic rule in wrongful dismissal is it is a contractual claim and so follows those principles which are to place him in the same position *as if the contract had been performed - Robinson v Harman [1848]*[xliii]. In *Boyo v Lambeth London Borough Council [1994]*[xliv] it was held that the correct measure of damages following the employer's repudiatory breach of contract was the amount the employee would be entitled to receive if dismissed in accordance with the terms of the contract. This will be the basis on which the damages are calculated for notice pay.

The other issue concerns Mario's dismissal apparently without following any proper disciplinary process. ACAS sets out clear guidelines on this in their <u>Code of Practice 1</u> on disciplinary and grievance procedures which his manager John Saltly should have followed the employer's procedure (assuming the employer as a well known university would follow as a matter of good practice). It appears in this case Mario was not given the opportunity to defend himself in a fair and transparent process, and therefore would be entitled to the income he would have earned if a proper disciplinary process had been followed *(Edwards v Chesterfield Royal Hospital NHS Foundation Trust*

[2009][xlv]*). This may require an estimation based on the timescales/time limits linked to the university disciplinary procedures.

In summary, Mario can be informed or advised that he is entitled to six month's notice pay (and any benefits accrued he may be entitled to under his contract – to be determined). He is however, under an obligation to try and mitigate his loss of salary and could have any award that is made reduced. In your discussions with Mario you would need to get information from him on his attempts to find another job (in practical terms copies of job applications, any other form of paid or volunteer work etc). Once his job was terminated he was under a duty to mitigate his loss and try to obtain suitable alternative employment. If he has not made any efforts to mitigate, his compensation award may be reduced. However, if he has tried and failed to find other suitable alternative employment, or has to work in a lower paid job, his damages could be more substantial.

Question

What is constructive dismissal?

Suggested answer

A constructive dismissal is where the conduct of the employer forces the employee to resign because the employer has committed a fundamental breach which goes to the root of the contract. In order for an employee to be said to be constructively dismissed within the statutory provisions, the employer's conduct must either be a significant breach going to the core of the contract, or prove that the employer will not continue to be bound by one or more of the essential terms of the contract. The employee can then rely on the principle that the contract has been discharged at common law *(Western Excavating Ltd v Sharp [1978]*[xlvi]*)*. An employee will only be entitled to treat him/herself as constructively dismissed if the employer is guilty of conduct that is a significant breach going to the root of the contract, or that shows that the employer no longer intends to be bound by one or more of its essential terms. If an employee continues to work for a length of time without leaving, they will be regarded as having affirmed the contract and lose the right to treat themselves as discharged. Conversely, if the employee makes clear their objection to what is being done then they are *not* considered to have affirmed the contract by continuing to work and get paid for a limited period. Section 95 of the ERA 96 gives a definition of constructive dismissal:-

- (1) For the purposes of this Part an employee is dismissed by his employer if …..
    - o (c) the employee terminates the contract under which he is employed (with or without notice) in circumstances in which he is entitled to terminate it without notice by reason of the employer's conduct.

Examples of repudiatory conduct are:-

- A unilateral reduction in pay by the employer including a reduction in fringe benefits *(Cantor Fitzgerald International v Callaghan & Others [1999]xlvii);*
- A fundamental change in the nature of the job such as a job description can amount to repudiation if there is no term allowing such a change *(Land Securities Trillium Ltd v Thornley [2005]xlviii);*
- Reducing the status of an employee by removing some of their duties and responsibilities *(Coleman v S&W Baldwin [1977]xlix;*
- Breach by the employer of the implied term not to*"conduct themselves in a manner calculated or likely to destroy or seriously damage the relationship of confidence and trust between the employer and employee"* (*Woods v WM Care Services (Peterborough) Ltd [1983]l).*

Problem question scenario

Constructive dismissal – Claim for constructive dismissal scenario

Barbara has worked at "Reds Pharmacy" as a pharmacist for five years. Three months ago she was told by the manager of the pharmacy, Greg Grey, she would from then on be expected to cover the cashier's general duties two days a week instead of dispensing pharmaceutical products at the pharmacy counter on those days (and hinted the other pharmacist had been more efficient at the job anyway). A month before that she had been asked to work an hour later than her contracted hours 3 evenings of the week which she objected to being asked to do but under protest had begrudgingly agreed to do. She protests against this latest order, particularly as it is not part of her job description or contract of employment. After a heated discussion with Greg, Barbara shouted she had had enough and said she was resigning stating she could not continue to work under these changed terms and walks out. Barbara comes to you for some help and advice. What advice would you offer her?

Suggested answer

There are a number of key documents you will need to examine closely in order to offer advice and support to Barbara, and conduct a case on her behalf. The documents are likely to include:-

- Contract of employment;
- Job description;
- Payment details, bonuses, reward package;
- Company handbook;
- Any other relevant correspondence between Barbara and her manager/human resources;

- Emails or documents regarding any informal or formal warnings or criticisms of her standard of work.

After discussing with Barbara her case and getting her version of events leading to her decision to resign from her job, you will need to scrutinize each of the documents. The documents will be crucial in informing any further action, and the nature of the advice to Barbara regarding the substance of her case.

If after a close examination of Barbara's employment contract the clause in her contract it is clear there is no express term enabling Greg Grey, her manager, to order her to work later in the evenings. This is then likely to amount to be a variation in her contract which he on behalf of the employer, cannot enforce unilaterally. However, if she can be said to have accepted the change it then becomes a lawful variation *(Jones v Associated Tunnelling Co Ltd [1981]*[li]*)*. In this scenario though Barbara appears to have made clear her resentment at having to work the extra hours so it can be argued she was working these extra hours under protest *(Burdett-Coutts v Hertfordshire County Council [1984]* [lii] *)*.
There may be the basis of an argument that her treatment amounts to a breach of the duty of mutual trust and confidence, implied into all contracts of employment. This duty requires both parties to act in a manner that does not seriously damage or destroy

the relationship between them *(Courtaulds Northern Textiles Ltd v Andrew [1979]*[liii]*).* There are examples of changes to Barbara's contract of employment which had a detrimental affect on her working conditions and environment. The requirement that Barbara work as a general cashier for two days a week rather than a pharmacist appears to be an attempt to undermine her status as a medical professional by reducing her status on those days *(Coleman v S&W Baldwin [1977]*[liv]*)* – reducing the status of an employee by removing some of their duties and responsibilities*).*

Finally there is the matter of the apparently throw away comments by Greg Grey that the other pharmacist was more effective at the job which appears to be a criticism of Barbara's work. This would also be evidence of behaviour by the manager/employer which undermines the employment relationship.

In summary, the series of events (extra hours, derogatory comments about her work and reduction of status) should be the basis for a case of constructive dismissal. The final incident may be argued as the "last straw" forcing her resignation *(Abbey National plc v Robinson [2000]*[lv]*).* You will need details of Barbara's pay and reward package to assess levels of compensation to argue for at the tribunal. This will be made up of the Basic Award and Compensation Award in the same way as unfair dismissal (with some differences). Barbara appears to the basis of an arguable case (bearing in mind all the caveats and clarification of the main points) that could be tested in court/tribunal with a reasonable chance of success (or compromise deal with the employer).

An example of the way this is calculated from the web:-

BASIC AWARD

The basic award is a statutory award that involves multiplying the relevant factors of the length of continuous service (up to a maximum of 20 years), your age and a week's pay (as at the effective date of termination) as follows:

- One and a half weeks' pay for each year of employment after age 41;
- One week's pay for each year of employment between ages 22 and 40;
- Half a week's pay for each year of employment under the age of 22.
  The weekly pay which will be used to work out the redundancy payment will usually be your normal weekly gross pay at the time you were dismissed up to the maximum limit which is **£525** from 6th April 2019). A week's pay does not usually include overtime pay. The maximum basic award payment you can receive is **£15,750.**

- A tribunal may reduce the basic award if it finds that your conduct before dismissal (or before notice of dismissal), was such that it would be *just and equitable* to reduce it- even if your conduct had not contributed to the dismissal.

If you have been dismissed by reason of **redundancy**, the tribunal will reduce the basic award by the amount of any redundancy payment you have received or awarded by the tribunal as part of the compensation. If, however, your employer fails to satisfy the tribunal that the principal reason for dismissal was in fact redundancy, then no such reduction to the basic award will be made.

COMPENSATORY AWARD

After addressing the basic award, the often, more larger compensatory award will then be considered. The Employment Rights Act provides that this will be *"such amount as the Tribunal considers just and equitable in all the circumstances having regard to the loss sustained by the complainant in consequence of the dismissal insofar as that loss is attributable to action taken by the employer"*.

Accordingly, the losses need to have arisen:
-as a consequence of the resignation;
-as a result of your employer's actions;
-and that it is just and equitable to make an award.
What are the main heads of losses that be claimed under a compensatory award?

These are:
- loss of wages;
- loss of future wages;
- loss of statutory rights (it takes 2 years before you have unfair dismissal protection, or you can qualify for a redundancy payment);
- loss of pension.

In terms of wages, this includes contractual benefits, such as a company car, private medical or health insurance. It can also include non-contractual benefits, provided you have a reasonable expectation of the same. You can also include a claim for your loss of **bonus** or commission if you reasonably expected to receive this, even if such payments were discretionary.

<u>Unlike in awards for unfair dismissal</u>, you must give credit when assessing your damages, for earnings you have received on what would have been your notice period. In other words, if you start another job, for example, within 1 month of leaving, and your notice period is 3 months, you can't claim for the further 2 month's notice within a constructive dismissal claim.
Assessing future loss is always going to be a speculative process for the tribunal, and will depend on whether you have managed to mitigate your loss and found another job before the hearing date, at what point, and the amount of your new salary. The tribunal will need to identify an appropriate cut-off point for compensation if you have not secured any new employment as at the hearing date.
The maximum amount that you can be awarded as compensation for Unfair Dismissal is presently the statutory cap of **£86,444**, or 52 weeks gross salary-whichever is the lower. This is in addition to the basic award which can be ordered by the Tribunal of up to a maximum of **£15,750**. These figures are from **6th April 2019**.

In calculating a year's salary, you do not take into account benefits in kind, pension contributions or discretionary bonuses.
Assuming you win your case, the tribunal will assess your total loss, and you will have to give credit for sums already received from your employer, such as pay in lieu of notice or enhanced redundancy payments.
https://www.landaulaw.co.uk

Problem question scenario

Unfair dismissal 3 – Claim for unfair dismissal

Ahmed is the manager or "Top trainers" sports shop. Jane is a member of staff who has worked in the shop for four years as a senior cashier. Jane saw a friend Mary walking past the shop and ran out to chat to her forgetting she had a brand new pair of expensive trainers in her hand. Sayed who also worked in the shop saw her and reported her to Ahmed saying he saw Jane give the trainers to Mary.

Ahmed called Jane into the office later in the afternoon and told her what Sayed had said. Jane denied Sayed's version of events and told Ahmed she had in fact taken the trainers back and two other members of staff (John and Sarah) had witnessed this. Ahmed did not believe Jane and did not bother to check with John and Sarah to get their version of what they witnessed.

Later that day Ahmed wrote a letter to Jane informing her of his decision to dismiss her for stealing the trainers and if she was unhappy with his decision she could write to Mr Jones the owner of "Top trainers" with her complaint.

Suggested answer

Jane has come to you for your advice. What would be your advice and/or guidance as a lawyer or legal professional?

After meeting with Jane and getting a clear understanding of the facts and her version of events. You would confirm in writing what was agreed at the meeting and how her case will be handled. It is important to clarify that Jane is still within the time limits for bring an unfair dismissal claim which is three months less one day. She has worked for "Top trainers" for over two years (check employment is continuous) so meets that criteria. If you are a Solicitor you would have to comply with Solicitors Regulation Authority (SRA) codes of conduct with certain information required in the letter set out below:-

Minimum requirements

The SRA Code of Conduct *You and Your Client* sets out the minimum information that should be included in CCLs, such as telling clients about:

• how their matter will be handled and their options

• the likely overall cost

• how complaints can be made to the firm and the Legal Ombudsman.

Based on SRA research on what clients want in terms of information found specific matters would be preferred to be included in the letter, such as:-

- a named contact

- scope of the agreed work

- fees and charges

- likely timescales

- details of next steps or any actions required.

https://www.sra.org.uk

Your advice or guidance for Jane based on the events set out in her situation could be –

- Ahmed the shop manager does not appear to have followed a fair process in dismissing her. He should have followed a company procedure the employer should have when dealing with cases involving disciplinary procedures.
- The ACAS Code of Practice 1 (COP) brought in under S.199 of the Trade Union and Labour

Relations (consolidation) Act 1992. In the introduction of the COP (paragraph 2) it states that *"Fairness and transparency are promoted by developing and using rules and procedures for handling disciplinary and grievance situations.* In goes on to say in paragraph 2 that the procedures and rules should be *"set down in writing, be specific and clear".* Ahmed does not seemed to have followed a process that meets this criteria which indicates the dismissal could be unfair.

- Paragraph 5 of the COP states that *"It is important to carry out necessary investigations of potential disciplinary matters without unreasonable delay to establish the facts of the case".* This includes the right to be informed of the allegations, invited to a hearing to rebut or defend herself against those charges/allegations, be accompanied by a fellow work/trade union representative, bring witnesses and set out reasonable timescales. Ahmed appears not to have done any of this before sending Jane a letter dismissing her, so is clearing a breach of the COP.

- The COP is not legally binding as such, but employment tribunals will take the Code into account when considering relevant cases. Any awards can be adjusted up by 25% for an employer who has unreasonably failed to follow the guidance within the Code. Ahmed has failed to follow this guidance so the company "Top trainers" could face paying more compensation for this failure (noting any "Polkey" *reduction - Polkey v A E Dayton Services [1987]*[lvi] if the employee was likely to have been dismissed anyway). A Polkey reduction looks unlikely based on the Jane's situation.

- Section 98(4) ERA 96 states that an employer must act reasonably in all the circumstances. The employment tribunal must reach a decision based on the principles or equity and the substantial merits of the case (*Iceland Frozen Foods v Jones [1983]*)[lvii].

- Ahmed on behalf of the employer may try to argue that the decision to dismiss Jane in the way he did falls within the "band of reasonable responses" but he would need to show his actions were fair and reasonable and this does not appear to be the case. There has been a complete failure to follow any kind of fair dismissal process with the basic principles of natural justice adhered to (supported above by relevant case law and statute) which is strong evidence of an unfair dismissal.

In summary Ahmed has acted unfairly in dismissing Jane. He has not followed any disciplinary procedure based around the *ACAS Code of Practice on Disciplinary and Grievance Procedures 2015*. The allegation against Jane is a very serious one as it involves theft and she should have been given the opportunity to defend herself bring witnesses (John and Sarah) as evidence she is not guilty of the charge. You should advise she consider issuing a claim within three months of her EDT (and advise her on the ACAS compulsory conciliation obligation). She could be entitled to financial compensation which consists of two elements:-

- The Basic Award current maximum is **£15,750**. (2019) based on a maximum week's pay of **£525**. A ready reckoner table is used for work out award.
- The Compensatory Award which currently has a maximum ceiling of **£86,444** (2019) or 52 weeks pay, whichever is the lower amount. This compensation covers actual costs she has incurred, including the estimation of future losses.

There are also remedies of re-instatement where Jane could return to her job (if re-instated) retaining her accrued benefits and service or re-engagement where she returns to her job basically as an employee starting again from scratch. Given the circumstance of her dismissal, compensation seems to favorable and appropriate remedy.

Question

What are the awards for unfair dismissal?

Suggested answer

The answer to this question is mainly given in suggested answer to the above problem question in relation to the monetary award which to recap is made up of two elements:-

1. BASIC AWARD

The basic award is a statutory award that involves multiplying the relevant factors of the length of continuous service (up to a maximum of 20 years), your age and a week's pay (as at the effective date of termination) as follows:

- One and a half weeks' pay for each year of employment after age 41;

- One week's pay for each year of employment between ages 22 and 40;

- Half a week's pay for each year of employment under the age of 22.
  The weekly pay which will be used to work out the redundancy payment will usually be your normal weekly gross pay at the time you were dismissed *up to the maximum limit* which is **£525** from 6th April 2019). A week's pay does not usually include overtime pay. The maximum basic award payment you can receive is **£15,240.**

- A tribunal may reduce the basic award if it finds that your conduct before dismissal (or before notice of dismissal), was such that it would be *just and equitable* to reduce it- even if your conduct had not contributed to the dismissal.

  If you have been dismissed by reason of *redundancy*, the tribunal will reduce the basic award by the amount of any redundancy payment you have received or awarded by the tribunal as part of the compensation. If, however, your employer fails to satisfy the tribunal that the principal reason for dismissal was in fact redundancy, then no such reduction to the basic award will be made.

2. COMPENSATORY AWARD

The compensatory award will be assessed next and is usually a more substantial compensatory award will then be considered.
Section 123(1) of the ERA 96 provides that this will be *"such amount as the Tribunal considers just and equitable in all the circumstances having regard to the loss sustained by the complainant in consequence of the dismissal insofar as that loss is attributable to action taken by the employer"*.

Thus the losses need to have come about:-

- o   as a consequence of the resignation;
- o   as a result of your employer's actions;
- o   and that it is just and equitable to make an award.

The main heads of losses that be claimed under a compensatory award are:-

- loss of wages;

- loss of future wages;

- loss of statutory rights (it takes 2 years before you have unfair dismissal protection, or you can qualify for a redundancy payment);

- loss of pension.

Wages will include contractual benefits, such as a company car, private medical or health insurance. It can also include non- contractual benefits, provided you have a reasonable expectation of the same. You can also include a claim for your loss of bonus or commission if you reasonably expected to receive this, even if such payments were discretionary.

When assessing future loss this will be a speculative process for the tribunal, and will depend on whether you have managed to *mitigate your loss* and found another job before the hearing date, at what point you found a job, and the amount of your new salary. The tribunal will need to identify an appropriate cut-off point for compensation if you have not secured any new employment *as at the hearing date.*

The maximum amount that you can be awarded as compensation for Unfair Dismissal is presently (2019) the statutory cap of **£86,444**, or 52 weeks gross salary- whichever is the lower. This is in addition to the basic award which can be ordered by the Tribunal of up to a maximum of **£15,750**. These figures are from 6th April 2019 and subject to annual upgrades.

In calculating a year's salary, you do not take into account benefits in kind, pension contributions or discretionary bonuses.

If you win your case, the tribunal will assess your total loss, and you will have to give credit for sums already received from your employer, such as pay in lieu of notice or enhanced redundancy payments.

Problem question scenario

Unfair dismissal 4 – Claim for unfair dismissal (monetary award)

Dhepa has come to you for help and advice with her unfair dismissal claim and you have successfully won her case. She now wants to know how her compensation will be worked out. Her hearing is listed six months after dismissal. She hopes to get a job on the same pay level soon. Can you produce a draft schedule of loss showing actual figures where possible, or an estimated calculation of the tribunal could use to base the award. She is 36 and worked for her previous employer, Golden Rail as a train driver for twelve years continuously before being unfairly dismissed.

Her remuneration information is:

- Gross annual salary = £36,000
- Net monthly pay = £2,500

- Annual bonus scheme = 6%
- Company car
- Private medical insurance
- Company pension scheme

SUGGESTED ANSWER

After checking all the information in Dhepa's pay and reward package you will need to start to make some calculations based on her remuneration package.

The first task is to work out her expected entitlement for her **Basic Award.** This is worked out using a ready reckoner table (example of table at the end of this section) to read across to work out a basic award. The same table is used for working out statutory redundancy pay.

Dheper's net monthly pay of £2,500 which would be above the maximum limit allowed for weekly pay which is currently capped at £525. Therefore her basic pay award would be based on this amount. She worked for her previous employer for twelve years – 12 x 525 = £6,300.

TOTAL - £6,300

That is the easy bit. The more complicated set of calculations will be more speculative which makes up the **Compensation Award.** This contains a number of elements and caveats. It is based on what is considered `just and equitable' so is discretionary. Looking at the various components:-

- Compensation of immediate loss – dismissal to date of hearing (say 3 months - 3 x £2,500 (net monthly pay) = £7,500;
- EDT to date of Hearing (say 6 months – 6 x £2,500 = £15,000 (note: Dhepa is under a duty to mitigate);
- Add Loss of pension benefits (say 5% of annual salary) – 5% of £36,000 = £1,800;
- Add Loss of fringe benefits – Use of company car for 3 months – say £500;
- Add Loss of health insurance – say £300;
- Add Loss of statutory rights – Usually around £300-£400 so say £300;
- NOTE – Current statutory cap on amounts payable on compensatory ward is maximum of £86,444 or 12 month's gross salary - £36,000 in Dhepa's case.

TOTAL - £25,400

TOTAL COMPENSATION + BASIC AWARD = £31,700

Reducing factors could be:-

- Any pay in Lieu – PILON (deducted from award
- Lack of mitigation – Attempts to find other suitable alternative employment

- ACAS COP – Unreasonable behavior of employee or employer can increase or reduce the award by 25%
- Contributory behavior – Did the employer contribute to the situation in any way?

The above are important factors to determine when giving help or advice on compensation awards.

The calculations used are very rough estimates or approximations. A detailed discussion with Dhepa and examination of all the relevant documents would need to be carried out to get more accurate figures (although there is still likely to be an element of estimation on compensation).

Age at termination	Complete years' service																				
	1	2	3	4	5	6	7	8	9	10	11	12	13	14	15	16	17	18	19	20
17	0.5	1	·	·	·	·	·	·	·	·	·	·	·	·	·	·	·	·	·	·
18	0.5	1	1.5	·	·	·	·	·	·	·	·	·	·	·	·	·	·	·	·	·
19	0.5	1	1.5	2	·	·	·	·	·	·	·	·	·	·	·	·	·	·	·	·
20	0.5	1	1.5	2	2.5	·	·	·	·	·	·	·	·	·	·	·	·	·	·	·
21	0.5	1	1.5	2	2.5	3	·	·	·	·	·	·	·	·	·	·	·	·	·	·
22	0.5	1	1.5	2	2.5	3	3.5	·	·	·	·	·	·	·	·	·	·	·	·	·
23	1	1.5	2	2.5	3	3.5	4	4.5	·	·	·	·	·	·	·	·	·	·	·	·
24	1	2	2.5	3	3.5	4	4.5	5	5.5	·	·	·	·	·	·	·	·	·	·	·
25	1	2	3	3.5	4	4.5	5	5.5	6	6.5	·	·	·	·	·	·	·	·	·	·
26	1	2	3	4	4.5	5	5.5	6	6.5	7	7.5	·	·	·	·	·	·	·	·	·
27	1	2	3	4	5	5.5	6	6.5	7	7.5	8	8.5	·	·	·	·	·	·	·	·
28	1	2	3	4	5	6	6.5	7	7.5	8	8.5	9	9.5	·	·	·	·	·	·	·
29	1	2	3	4	5	6	7	7.5	8	8.5	9	9.5	10	10.5	·	·	·	·	·	·
30	1	2	3	4	5	6	7	8	8.5	9	9.5	10	10.5	11	11.5	·	·	·	·	·
31	1	2	3	4	5	6	7	8	9	9.5	10	10.5	11	11.5	12	12.5	·	·	·	·
32	1	2	3	4	5	6	7	8	9	10	10.5	11	11.5	12	12.5	13	13.5	·	·	·
33	1	2	3	4	5	6	7	8	9	10	11	11.5	12	12.5	13	13.5	14	14.5	·	·
34	1	2	3	4	5	6	7	8	9	10	11	12	12.5	13	13.5	14	14.5	15	15.5	·
35	1	2	3	4	5	6	7	8	9	10	11	12	13	13.5	14	14.5	15	15.5	16	16.5
36	1	2	3	4	5	6	7	8	9	10	11	12	13	14	14.5	15	15.5	16	16.5	17
37	1	2	3	4	5	6	7	8	9	10	11	12	13	14	15	15.5	16	16.5	17	17.5
38	1	2	3	4	5	6	7	8	9	10	11	12	13	14	15	16	16.5	17	17.5	18
39	1	2	3	4	5	6	7	8	9	10	11	12	13	14	15	16	17	17.5	18	18.5
40	1	2	3	4	5	6	7	8	9	10	11	12	13	14	15	16	17	18	18.5	19
41	1	2	3	4	5	6	7	8	9	10	11	12	13	14	15	16	17	18	19	19.5
42	1.5	2.5	3.5	4.5	5.5	6.5	7.5	8.5	9.5	10.5	11.5	12.5	13.5	14.5	15.5	16.5	17.5	18.5	19.5	20.5
43	1.5	3	4	5	6	7	8	9	10	11	12	13	14	15	16	17	18	19	20	21
44	1.5	3	4.5	5.5	6.5	7.5	8.5	9.5	10.5	11.5	12.5	13.5	14.5	15.5	16.5	17.5	18.5	19.5	20.5	21.5
45	1.5	3	4.5	6	7	8	9	10	11	12	13	14	15	16	17	18	19	20	21	22
46	1.5	3	4.5	6	7.5	8.5	9.5	10.5	11.5	12.5	13.5	14.5	15.5	16.5	17.5	18.5	19.5	20.5	21.5	22.5
47	1.5	3	4.5	6	7.5	9	10	11	12	13	14	15	16	17	18	19	20	21	22	23
48	1.5	3	4.5	6	7.5	9	10.5	11.5	12.5	13.5	14.5	15.5	16.5	17.5	18.5	19.5	20.5	21.5	22.5	23.5
49	1.5	3	4.5	6	7.5	9	10.5	12	13	14	15	16	17	18	19	20	21	22	23	24
50	1.5	3	4.5	6	7.5	9	10.5	12	13.5	14.5	15.5	16.5	17.5	18.5	19.5	20.5	21.5	22.5	23.5	24.5
51	1.5	3	4.5	6	7.5	9	10.5	12	13.5	15	16	17	18	19	20	21	22	23	24	25
52	1.5	3	4.5	6	7.5	9	10.5	12	13.5	15	16.5	17.5	18.5	19.5	20.5	21.5	22.5	23.5	24.5	25.5
53	1.5	3	4.5	6	7.5	9	10.5	12	13.5	15	16.5	18	19	20	21	22	23	24	25	26
54	1.5	3	4.5	6	7.5	9	10.5	12	13.5	15	16.5	18	19.5	20.5	21.5	22.5	23.5	24.5	25.5	26.5
55	1.5	3	4.5	6	7.5	9	10.5	12	13.5	15	16.5	18	19.5	21	22	23	24	25	26	27
56	1.5	3	4.5	6	7.5	9	10.5	12	13.5	15	16.5	18	19.5	21	22.5	23.5	24.5	25.5	26.5	27.5
57	1.5	3	4.5	6	7.5	9	10.5	12	13.5	15	16.5	18	19.5	21	22.5	24	25	26	27	28
58	1.5	3	4.5	6	7.5	9	10.5	12	13.5	15	16.5	18	19.5	21	22.5	24	25.5	26.5	27.5	28.5
59	1.5	3	4.5	6	7.5	9	10.5	12	13.5	15	16.5	18	19.5	21	22.5	24	25.5	27	28	29
60	1.5	3	4.5	6	7.5	9	10.5	12	13.5	15	16.5	18	19.5	21	22.5	24	25.5	27	28.5	29.5
61+	1.5	3	4.5	6	7.5	9	10.5	12	13.5	15	16.5	18	19.5	21	22.5	24	25.5	27	28.5	30

Example or ready reckoner table for calculating pay in Basic Award

Useful guidance found on the CAB website as well:-
https://www.citizensadvice.org.uk/work/leaving-a-job/redundancy/redundancy-pay/

Problem question scenario

Unfair dismissal 5 – Claim for unfair dismissal (monetary award 2)

Mary is 26 years and had worked in "Grey's shoe express" shop continually for 10 years before being unfairly dismissed in November 2018 and her gross basic week's pay in her last week was £400. Mary has come to you after winning her case to explain how her basic pay award will be calculated and what is her award likely to be?

SUGGESTED ANSWER

This scenario requires you to vary your calculation to take account of the slightly different age range. The age factor in Mary's situation will affect the interpretation of the amount she is likely to be entitled to.

This is likely to be the way her basic award is calculated:-

- 1 x 4 x £400 = £1,600 (i.e. for ages 22, 23,24, 25)
- ½ x 6 x £400 = £1,200 (i.e. for ages 21,20,19,18,17,16)

Total (basic award) = £2,800

It is important to show Mary how her award is calculated using the ready reckoner. She needs to be able to understand how her age is a big factor in the calculation of the award. From age 22-25 she will be entitled to the complete yearly amount of her final week's pay (in her case £400) for each year worked. However for the years she has worked up until age 21 she will only be entitled to ½ a week's gross salary (£200) for those earlier years (see the ready reckoner).

ABOUT THE AUTHOR

I have studied law for many years as a part time student and have both undergraduate and post graduate qualifications and have completed the LPC. I have worked in volunteer legal support roles offering advice and assistance in mainly employment law related roles. I was a trade union senior caseworker and negotiator dealing with employment related matters. I maintain a keen interest in legal issues in particular, as well as other areas of study.

INDEX

List of Statutes/Regulations

Employment Rights Act 1996

Employment Act 2002

National Minimum Wage Act 1998

Working Time Regulations 1998

Health and Safety at Work Act 1974

Management of Health and Safety at Work Regulations 1992 (MHSWR)

The Manual Handling Operations Regulations 1992 ,

The Supply of Machinery (Safety) Regulations 1992 (Machinery Regulations)

The Workplace (Health, Safety and Welfare) Regulations 1992

Part-time Workers (Prevention of Less Favourable Treatment) Regulations 2000

Fixed-term Employees (Prevention of Less Favourable Treatment) Regulations) 2002

Enterprise and Regulatory Reform Act 2013

Employment Tribunals (Early Conciliation: Exemptions and Rules of Procedure) Regulations 2014

List of Cases

Alboni (Respondent) v Ind Coope Retail Ltd [1998] IRLR 131

Autoclenz Ltd v Belcher [2011] IRLR 820

Barber v Somerset County Council: [2004] 1 All ER 737

Barnes v Gilmartin Association [1998] UKEAT/825/97

BG plc v O'Brien [2001] IRLR 496

Boyo v Lambeth London Borough Council [1994] ICR 727

British Home Stores v Burchell [1978] IRLR 379

Burdett-coutts v Hertfordshire County Council [1984] IRLR 91

Burns v Santander Plc [2011] UKEAT/0500/10/RN

Cairns v Visteon UK Ltd UKEAT/0494/06/JOJ

Cantor Fitzgerald International v Callaghan & Others [1999] IRLR 234

Carmichael v National Power Plc [1999] UKHL 47

Coleman v S&W Baldwin [1977] IRLR 342

Coleman v S&W Baldwin [1977] IRLR 342

Courtaulds Northern Textiles Ltd v Andrew [1979] IRLR 84

Crowson Fabrics Ltd v Rider and Others [2007] IRLR 288 ChD

Dacas v Brooke Street Bureau [2004] IRLR 358 (CA)

Edwards v Chesterfield Royal Hospital NHS Foundation Trust [2009] UKSC 58

Express and Echo Publications v Tanton [1999]

Faccenda Chicken Ltd v Fowler [1986] Ch 117

Foot v Eastern Counties Timber Co Ltd [1972] IRLR 83b IT

GM Gorfin v Distressed Gentlefolks Aid Association [1973] IRLR 290

Hilton v Shiner Builders Merchants [2002] UKHL 23

Hivac Ltd v Park Royal Scientific Instruments Ltd [1946]

Hollister v National Farmers Union [1979] ICR 542 [1979] IRLR 238

Imam-Sadeque v Blue Bay Asset Management (Services) Ltd [2012] EWHC 3511 (QB)

Jackson v Liverpool City Council [2011] CA 15

James v London Borough of Greenwich [2008] EWCA Civ 35

Jones v Associated Tunnelling co Ltd [1981] IRLR 477 EAT

Land Securities Trillium Ltd v Thornley [2005] IRLR 765

Latimer v AEC Ltd [1953] AC 643 (HL)

Laws v London Chronicle Ltd [1959] All ER 285

Lister v Romford Ice and Cold Storage Co Ltd [1957] AC 555

MacFarlane v Glasgow City Council [2000] EAT 1277/99/1705

Malik v BCCI [1997] UKHL

Morrow v Safeway Stores Plc [2002] EAT 21

Paris v Stepney Borough Council [1951] AC 367 (HL)

Pimlico Plumbers Ltd v Smith [2018] UKSC 29

Robb v Green [1895] 2 QB 1

Robinson v Harman [1848] 1 Ex 850

Roger Bullivant Ltd v Ellis [1987] EWCA Civ J0523-2

Sanders v Parry [1967] 1 WLR 753

Secretary of State for Employment v ASLEF (No 2) [1972] 2 All ER 949 CA

Spence v Department of Agriculture and Rural Development [2011] IRLR 806

Spring v Guardian Assurance Plc [1994] UKHL 7

Sterling v United Learning Trust [2015] UKEAT/0439/14/DM

The Moorcock [1881] 14 PD 64

United Bank Ltd v Akhtar [1989] IRLR 507

Walker v Northumberland County Council [1995] 1 All ER 737

Western Excavating Ltd v Sharp [1978]ICR 221 CA

Wilson & Clyde Coal Co Ltd v English [1938] AC 643 (HL)

Woods v WM Care Services (Peterborough) Ltd [1983] IRLR 413 (CA)

[i] www.pearsoned.co.uk/lawexpress

[ii] Carmichael v National Power Plc [1999] UKHL 47
[iii] Express and Echo Publications v Tanton [1999]
[iv] MacFarlane v Glasgow City Council [2000] EAT 1277/99/1705
[v] Dacas v Brooke Street Bureau [2004] IRLR 358 (CA)
[vi] Cairns v Visteon UK Ltd UKEAT/0494/06/JOJ
[vii] James v London Borough of Greenwich [2008] EWCA Civ 35

[ix] Autoclenz Ltd v Belcher [2011] IRLR 820
[x] Pimlico Plumbers Ltd v Smith [2018] UKSC 29
[xi] The Moorcock [1881] 14 PD 64
[xii] Burns v Santander Plc [2011] UKEAT/0500/10/RN
[xiii] Malik v BCCI [1997] UKHL
[xiv] Morrow v Safeway Stores Plc [2002] EAT 21
[xv] Hilton v Shiner Builders Merchants [2002] UKHL 23
[xvi] BG Plc v O'Brien [2001] IRLR 496 EAT
[xvii] United Bank Ltd v Akhtar [1989] IRLR 507
[xviii] Paris v Stepney Borough Council [1951] AC 367 (HL)
[xix] Latimer v AEC Ltd [1953] AC 643 (HL)
[xx] Walker v Northumberland County Council [1995] 1 All ER 737
[xxi] Wilson & Clyde Coal Co Ltd v English [1938] AC 643 (HL)
[xxii] Barber v Somerset County Council: [2004] 1 All ER 737
[xxiii] Spring v Guardian Assurance Plc [1994] UKHL 7
[xxiv] Jackson v Liverpool City Council [2011] CA 15
[xxv] Laws v London Chronicle Ltd [1959] All ER 285
[xxvi] Secretary of State for Employment v ASLEF (No 2) [1972] 2 All ER 949 CA
[xxvii] Lister v Romford Ice and Cold Storage Co Ltd [1957] AC 555
[xxviii] Crowson Fabrics Ltd v Rider and Others [2007] IRLR 288 ChD

[xxix] Imam-Sadeque v Blue Bay Asset Management (Services) Ltd [2012] EWHC 3511 (QB)

[xxx] Hivac Ltd v Park Royal Scientific Instruments Ltd [1946]

[xxxi] Roger Bullivant Ltd v Ellis [1987] EWCA Civ J0523-2

[xxxii] Robb v Green [1895] 2 QB 1

[xxxiii] Sanders v Parry [1967] 1 WLR 753

[xxxiv] Faccenda Chicken Ltd v Fowler [1986] Ch 117

[xxxv] Spence v Department of Agriculture and Rural Development [2011] IRLR 806

[xxxvi] British Home Stores v Burchell [1978] IRLR 379

[xxxvii] GM Gorfin v Distressed Gentlefolks Aid Association [1973]

[xxxviii] Foot v Eastern Counties Timber Co Ltd [1972] IRLR 83b IT

[xxxix] Alboni (Respondent) v Ind Coope Retail Ltd [1998] IRLR 131

[xl] Barnes v Gilmartin Association [1998] UKEAT/825/97

[xli] Hollister v National Farmers Union [1979] ICR 542 [1979] IRLR 238

[xlii] Sterling v United Learning Trust [2015] UKEAT/0439/14/DM

[xliii] Robinson v Harman [1848] 1 Ex 850

[xliv] Boyo v Lambeth London Borough Council [1994] ICR 727

[xlv] Edwards v Chesterfield Royal Hospital NHS Foundation Trust [2009] UKSC 58

[xlvi] Western Excavating Ltd v Sharp [1978]ICR 221 CA

[xlvii] Cantor Fitzgerald International v Callaghan & Others [1999] IRLR 234

[xlviii] Land Securities Trillium Ltd v Thornley [2005] IRLR 765

[xlix] Coleman v S&W Baldwin [1977] IRLR 342

[l] Woods v WM Care Services (Peterborough) Ltd [1983] IRLR 413 (CA)

[li] Jones v Associated Tunnelling co Ltd [1981] IRLR 477 EAT

[lii] Burdett-coutts v Hertfordshire County Council [1984] IRLR 91

[liii] Courtaulds Northern Textiles Ltd v Andrew [1979] IRLR 84

[liv] Coleman v S&W Baldwin [1977] IRLR 342

[lv] Abbey National Plc v Robinson [2000]) All ER (D) 1884

[lvi] Polkey v A E Dayton Services [1987] UKHL 8

[lvii] Iceland Frozen Foods Ltd v Jones [1983] ICR 17

Printed in Great Britain
by Amazon